NEW MEN — DEEPER HUNGERS

NEW MEN

●

DEEPER HUNGERS

by
TOM OWEN-TOWLE

Cover Artwork by TONY SHEETS
Graphics by DAVID STARY-SHEETS

SUNFLOWER INK
Palo Colorado Canyon   Carmel, Calif. 93923

IN MEMORIAM:
HAROLD ALEXANDER TOWLE

(January 29, 1906–December 24, 1987)

Last Christmas eve, between the Vespers and Midnight services, my father died.

Not a formally religious man, Dad nourished his spirit by being an overflowingly generous person as well as a gifted guitarist who played his heart inside out (he had a New Year's eve gig planned when he died).

I am blessed to carry on both legacies: a day does not go by without my trying to emulate my father's generous nature, and I humbly travel with his 1937 Gibson, playing it every chance I get. I can hear him singing whenever I strum.

Dad and I never talked about men's issues or what it means to be a man. He just *was* one—the best version he knew how to be, and by example, not word, invited me to follow suit.

Dad never understood my fascination with theological matters. He was a doer rather than a seeker. He didn't play with imponderables. He would not have shown interest in the concerns of intimacy *and* ultimacy which fill the following pages.

So this book isn't his story, but he raised a son whose story it is. I fantasize Dad reading it, along with recent copies of *The Sporting News,* sitting on the throne late at night.

He would read my book only because his boy wrote it, and anything his sons did made him unspeakably proud.

The feeling is mutual, Dad.

I have waited fifteen years for this book. After reviewing an early draft, I asked Tom Owen-Towle if I could write the foreword. As a psychologist, I have long recognized the need for a book that would touch men's hearts, while appealing to our growing desire for self-understanding. This book is it.

I have read everything I could get my hands on about contemporary men and their relationships. Something was always missing. My own book was as much a stylistic attempt to provide this missing piece as it was a documentary about men's inner lives. But only recently, after reading *NEW MEN—DEEPER HUNGERS*, did I realize what else was missing. From the moment I picked up this book, I felt like it had been written for me. Tom has hit the jackpot. He has found a tone of voice in which to speak to men's hearts. How is this possible?

Very few men could have written this book. Tom Owen-Towle is a man who is as easy and engaging to read as he is to listen to. He gets to the proverbial bottom line effortlessly, calling into play a refreshingly updated look at the practical and spiritual wisdom of the ages. Tom's style delights and his stories fascinate.

Perhaps, years from now, the thing that will most distinguish this book is that hundreds of thousands of men will actually have picked it up, and read it. Sure, they will feel deeply understood and affirmed reading it, and the women in their lives will learn tremendously from it as well. But the amazing thing is that men will want to read this book. And that will be a first.

Market researchers tell us that women constitute about 85% of the book-buying public. Virtually all of the books about men are written for women and have in common a tone of blame: men are at fault for women's unhappiness and dissatisfaction. Such volumes leave out the majority of men and women—people who are honestly searching for tools to build rather than blame.

The success of Tom's book will prove that men want to understand and be understood—the same as women.

It is a rare and precious jewel of a book that Tom Owen-Towle has presented us all.

Ken Druck, Ph.D
Author of *THE SECRETS MEN KEEP*

INTRODUCTION

*"You are what your deep, driving
desire is. As your deep, driving
desire is, so is your will. As
your will is, so is your deed.
As your deed is, so is your destiny."*

The Upanishads

The story goes that Sigmund Freud developed a head-ache after counseling a female client. He took to his couch, and lying there, muttered under his breath: "What do women really want?"

Well, the same question is now being asked of today's men: "What do they really want?" It is raised out of curiosity, affection, and exasperation. Women and children aren't the only questioners. We men are also asking ourselves: "What are my deep, driving desires? What do I truly want from my days on this planet?"

The popular view contends that American males are driven by three basic desires: sex, money, and power. This book portrays a different, new breed of men who exhibit deeper hungers than this classic trio.

While not speaking for all men (who can?), these adult males represent a growing constituency in our land. They are open, sensitive men who struggle to shed stereotypes en route to birthing a masculinity marked by flexibility, joy, pain, firmness, and depth.

Although the following essays were composed primarily *about* and *for* men, women are encouraged to listen in

ix

and learn firsthand what's going on in the hearts of the new men who live next to them during work, at play, in friendship, and in love.

What exactly do new men seek? For what do we yearn?

We want healthier ways of relating to women, other men, and the children in our lives.

We want work large enough to stretch our minds and touch our hearts.

We want male support so that we can exchange delights, wounds, impasses, and longings in a safe, caring atmosphere.

We want to quit having to prove ourselves at the office, in bed, and on the playing field so that we can begin to let go, relax, and reveal our true selves.

We want to be strong but not macho, gentle without being wimpish, vulnerable without falling prey to self-pity, both needy and self-reliant, expressive rather than emotionally constricted, more spiritually awake.

We want to be mature enough that we don't always have to seem mature.

We want to grow bolder as we age: shedding habits, taking risks, claiming our rights.

New men want to be playful, climb off the ladder, celebrate our God, confront our fears, find rest and renewal, forgive and be forgiven, learn from the animals, feel less miserable, unclench our fists, open our tear-ducts, face our own mortality, leave a lasting legacy, and much more.

In sum, we new men are no longer satisfied with acquisitions and awards; we crave meaning and fulfillment as well.

NEW MEN—DEEPER HUNGERS depicts men engaged in a lifelong quest to fill our bedrock hopes and desires.

WE WANT

We Want...

I *We want*
TO BE BORNE AGAIN

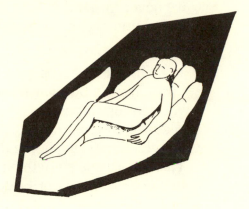

"Moses' father-in-law said to him, 'What you are doing is not good. You and the people with you will wear yourselves out, for the thing is too heavy for you; you are not able to perform it alone. Moreover, choose able ones from all the people . . . they will bear the burden with you."

Exodus 18: 17-22

One of my fondest memories as a child was being carried about on my parents' shoulders or being cradled in their laps. I felt safe, secure, and loved.

This nurturing seldom happens to men when we grow older. Yet we hanker to relive our early experiences of being held, lifted, caressed, yes, carried. We

1

are socialized as males to climb over and around other men and women rather than climb into one another's arms. But we never forget the warmth and support of our primary holdings. We never lose the need.

One of the ways men avoid facing this hunger is by always carrying others. We bear up under any and all conditions. We take care of our partners, support our children, bring home the bread. There is always something or someone to be borne upon our burly shoulders. We fail to admit *our* desire to be carried by someone else—not only physically, but emotionally and spiritually as well.

I urge us men to pay heed to Jethro's advice to Moses, his son-in-law, to quit doing everything by himself and to invite others to share the responsibilities of his quest. When Moses turned for help, he learned that his burdens were cut in half.

My friend Dick says that we men are healthiest when we say, "I'm afraid," "Help me," "Hold me." For in that very saying will emerge renewed strength.

The true size of a man is directly proportional to his willingness to ask for another's hand or arm—to be borne again and again and again.

2

II *We want*
TO HAVE BUDDIES

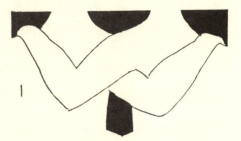

In the recent movie *Stand by Me,* based on Stephen King's novella, several young boys embark on a wild escapade to locate a dead body. The movie depicts the affectionate, competitive interplay among the boys as they engage in this scary adventure.

At the end, the narrator laments: "Life never gets this good anymore. We spend our entire adult lives trying to recapture the excitement and bond of being boys together, but we fail to do so."

Most men leave behind male buddies in their teens. As one wit put it, "In American life it seems as though you've got to have a bosom to be a buddy." What an unfortunate twist of gender, because the word "buddy" has been a baby talk alternative of "brother" since the early 1900's.

3

Things seem to be opening up for men today; rather men are opening themselves up. Some of us are pursuing closer friendships through playing, eating, hiking, singing, and talking together with other men. New men covet buddies not only when swimming in deep water but also when sharing deep thoughts and feelings.

In the German language, childhood peers, family members, and dear adult friends are affectionately addressed "Du" rather than "Sie." I will never forget the power of the "Duzen" ceremony when my newly developing German friend, Michael, invited me to drink a toast to our kinship with the word "bruderschaft."

We were evolving from associates to buddies. I regret our bond hasn't lasted through the intervening two decades, but I have sworn bruderschaft since with other men, and such friendships have enlarged me.

Lawrence stood up in the middle of our men's discussion group one night and said:

"I've got a personal announcement to make. Leonard has come into my life as a good, no make that a dear, friend. I have a buddy now,

4

something I can't remember having since boy scouts. I feel a happiness hard to express. Cheers for us, and may a similar delight happen to the rest of you men somewhere along the path."

There is a little boy in every adult male, and that youngster remains lonely until he finds a pal.

III *We want*
TO LOAF
AND INVITE OUR SOULS

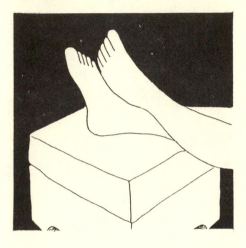

"I loaf and invite my soul. I lean and loaf at my ease observing a spear of summer grass."

Walt Whitman

There is no more common complaint in the overstressed, adult male world than being winded, bushed, bone-tired, out of breath. Nathan remarked: "As a teenager I joined the rat race, being a boxboy after school, and I haven't stopped running. I'm beat. I'm about to turn the race over to the rats. I need rest!"

Loafing is not a luxury but a necessity for men. We can't leave our relaxing to chance; it must be built into each day's flow. Rest might entail taking a nap, doing yoga, meditating by oneself in a quiet garden, or walking.

I hear men complain: "Hey, I can't fit one more thing on to my agenda; I'm pooped." I reply, "Being pooped puts you precisely in the proper state to stop, catch you breath, rest, and get a second wind."

Our male tendency, however, is to work until we drop, then enter a "crash" relaxation program. Or we hang on until our vacation arrives (during which time some of us lug around our briefcases anyway). As John confided: "I always try to waste time in the most profitable way—even in Hawaii." Rest is seen by too many of us as a last resort.

The new male hungers to live intensely but not tensely. He takes regular breaks during the day. He ends each day with good exhaustion, a sense of having been well used. He takes a bona fide day off per week—in short, he honors the sabbath, to keep it holy and himself healthy. He knows that minutes of rest each day will add years of serenity to his life.

As in music, he believes a rest, the

pause between notes, is integral to the overall piece of music being composed.

Fred takes naps without feeling guilty.

Dwayne has a massage every other week because it is one of the few times he is passive and receiving.

Sam engages each day in a playful activity, doing what the monks have wisely called "deliberate irrelevancies."

Orloff knows that his work is so meaningful that he must save some of it for tomorrow rather than cram it all into today.

Henry Cadbury, the Quaker biblical authority, tells about a small boy who, when asked which story in the Bible he liked best, replied: "Oh, you know, that one about the multitude who fish and loaf. . ." Now there's sound doctrine for frenzied men.

My dear brothers, take a break before you are broken. Several of them. Daily.

IV *We want*
TO GROW MORE TENDER

"Joseph was so full of tender feelings that he had to control himself."

Genesis 43: 31

Sam Keen and James Fowler in their volume, *Life-Maps,* describe two kinds of demons in our culture: the marshmallow demons and the fire demons. They urge us to balance "both fierceness and tenderness, discipline and love, moderation and excess" in our pursuit of full humanness.

The world is looking for men who are versatile, balanced, ambidextrous. The problem is we are taught to be primarily tough and strong. We must pick up, later on, how to tend to feelings

9

and others, to speak tenderly, to be tender persons.

Anyone can run the risk of extremism, thus driving a virtue into the ground. If we men are overly tender, what is called "wimpish" today, then we end up spineless. We must never cease to be aggressive against injustice, forceful against wrong, stout-hearted in multiple ways. But most men will have to go a long way before they suffer from too much tenderness.

The male tragedy, as with Joseph in the Old Testament, is that once we begin to show our gentle side, we tend to tighten up, shut down our tender sentiments, control ourselves.

We men already know how to be hard-nosed, hard-at-work, play hard-ball; we want to grow more tender, and stay more mellow.

We would do well to meditate upon the ancient wisdom of the Chinese philosopher, Lao-Tzu:

> "All living growth is pliant until death transfixes it. Thus men who have hardened are 'kin of death.' And men who stay soft are 'kin of life.'"

V *We want* TO BE PLAYFUL

"Why has play become the opposite of seriousness? It did not start out as such; it began as a natural way of being."

David Miller

Before children can read a single word, they build with blocks, show great imagination, run, hop, swing—the kinds of things we adults hanker to do.

Some of the smart new men I know are rediscovering the joys of playfulness. They eschew the old Protestant work ethic which dictates that "you can work or you can have fun, but you can't do both." Baloney! Numbers of men are combining both with gusto. As my colleague Richard says: "There's no reason why we men can't practice the *work* ethic along with the *shirk* ethic."

Men are realizing that anyone with a body is inescapably an athlete and are engaging in competitive and non-competitive games which fit their desires—playing for the sake of playfulness. We are tired of being couch potatoes.

Ken made a personal breakthrough when he understood that he didn't have to *make* play; he could have fun simply by being spontaneous. He is now gaining a flair for the serendipitous: the art of finding valuable or fun things not sought. When he goes on walks, he takes detours, talks to passersby, examines plants, picks up interesting objects along the path, skips.

Douglas invited a group of men over to his house for lunch on a Saturday. Lego blocks were piled on each man's placemat. We were asked to play, alone and collectively, with the toys before we shared our food. We had a blast!

The zaniest display of uninhibited play I know of is done by my friend Dana, who takes his magic cards and bubbleblower with him wherever he goes. He has occasionally, in the middle of a difficult or boring meeting, pulled out his

12

fun-making tools and put on a tension-breaking display.

One of my models for balanced behavior has been the famous peace activist, A. J. Muste. Unlike some driven, dreamy-eyed idealists, Muste was naturally playful.

Colman McCarthy tells of a young disciple's first meeting with the master. "A. J. Muste walked in. I thought of his past revolutionary activities and his fierce bravery in laboring for a world with peace. I waited with great anticipation for his first word. A. J. looked around, and inquired, 'How did the Dodgers make out yesterday?' I was shocked."

I was thrilled to hear that Muste was a man who could balance both pleasure and challenge, labor and play, and all the combinations thereof.

We need such men in our fold. Real men, mature men, ambidextrous men like A. J. Muste.

VI *We want*
TO WALK BESIDE WOMEN

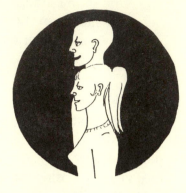

"Don't walk in front of me—I may not follow. Don't walk behind me—I may not lead. Walk beside me and just be my friend."

Albert Camus

"The times, they are a-changin'", as Bob Dylan used to croon. That truth is no more evident than in relationships between men and women.

In some cases dominant men are grudgingly relinquishing leadership in the political and business worlds. But a growing number of men are enthusiastic about equal sharing of the parental or economic load, because they are thereby freed to explore new zones of feeling and being as women pursue fresh ways of doing and producing.

14

Down deep the new male is weary of being in charge, leading all the time. Nor are we interested in being full-time followers. The dance that works best is when men and women move alongside one another, seldom focusing on who leads or follows but dancing on. A mutually pleasurable dance is what matters.

The sexes are in transition. Women are breaking out of Cinderella complexes and men out of John Wayne syndromes as we all scramble toward more gratifying personhood and companionship.

Men and women do this courageously but imperfectly. I was struck by a cartoon showing a man and woman sitting down to eat a lovely dinner together. One said to the other: "We're not perfect for each other, but then we're not perfect for anyone else either."

We need to handle one another with utmost care, with patience yet nudging, with a firm but flexible and forgiving hand. Women are getting in touch with their independence and men with their dependence. We're both on a road moving toward interdependence.

Not forfeiting our own pressing needs and aspirations, we men and women want to grow *human* liberation, the only form of liberation large enough for the whole enterprise. Our vision is not only to be freed *from* our unique bondages but also to be freed *for* mutual bonds of nurturance and fulfillment.

Although many women and men are able to garner liberal attitudes, few are ready or willing to engage in liberated living alongside one another. That's the litmus test, the full human call.

I think Eugene put his finger on the key to effective human relations when he offered: "We need to change one letter in our encounters with the opposite gender: more collusion and less collision."

VII *We want*
TO AVOID RUTS

*"It is not true that life is
one damn thing after another.
It is one damn thing over and
over."*

Edna St. Vincent Millay

As the sign on a muddy road in
Tennessee states: "Choose your rut
carefully because you will be in it for the
next twenty miles." Or should we amend
that to read, twenty *years*? Ruts, when
well, worn, become deep ditches.

We men get into various kinds of
ruts: sexual patterns, daily grinds, job
binds. We show little imagination. Our
adventurous natures are showcased
when we go river-rafting once a year.
Then we crawl back into our ruts upon
return.

A common male refrain is: "I'll do what I really want to do when I retire." Then, of course, we retire and forget what our desires are, or we are too fatigued to pursue anything new or interesting.

Now is the time to break out of boring grooves—to shed this, weigh that, venture something novel.

What we need are routes not ruts, direction not ditches. Get bolder, men, as you grow older.

VIII *We want*
TO SHUT UP AND LISTEN

"If it is language that makes us human, one half of language is to listen. Silence can exist without speech, but speech cannot live without silence. Listen to the speech of others. Listen even more to their silences."

Jacob Trapp

At a time when women are unleashing strong, forceful voices, men are learning to quiet down, even stop talking altogether.

Remember that Elijah did not locate God in the earthquake or the wind or the fire, the normal ways in his era for theophanies, but in "a still, small voice" or as one translator phrases it, "the sound of a soft stillness."

Mary pondered things in her heart

says the New Testament. Whether Joseph, her husband, did or not, he would have benefited from "going into the silence" as well. We males are trained to be center stage, blurt out, dominate, overtalk, especially in the presence of women. It's not too late for us to learn new ways, to develop the craft of active listening.

I appreciate the rhythm poet Joseph Lonero urges:

"Listen, he says. I want to tell you about myself. Hurry, she says. I've got a story too."

In men's groups one of our primary rules is the right to reticence. No one has to open his mouth in order to be a fully valued, contributing member of the fellowship.

Gandhi set an inspiring example by taking an entire day each week for silence. He did this to recharge his spiritual batteries. He would enjoy nature, meditate, play, but he wouldn't utter a sound.

New men try to set aside thirty minutes per day in which to shut up and do nothing but listen.

IX We want
TO FEEL
LESS MISER-ABLE

It is no surprise that men often feel miserable. Look at the word; the hyphen tells the story: miser-able. Because we are stingy with our affections, tight with our time, pinched with our feelings, we fall prey to misery. The first dictionary definition of "miser" is "a wretched person."

Remember J. Alfred Prufrock in T.S. Eliot's poem: "I have measured out my life with coffee spoons..." How sad! One of the areas where hard-working men tend to be miserly is with respect to our daily work schedules. We are governed, even tyrannized, by our datebooks. Doctors stack up patients in the waiting room. Businessmen are obsessed with meeting deadlines to generate more money.

The yuppie slogan, "The man with the most toys wins," has been a seductive ploy to weasel men into greater work frenzy. The truth is that the more toys we pile up, the more toys we want. The cycle is endless. We work, we buy; we toil, we buy...then we wear out, we lose, we die. Unfulfilled.

King Midas adored wealth. His obsession was granted: everything he touched turned to gold. But it backfired because his daughter became a golden statue, and his food wasn't edible—it was gold.

The only cure for avarice or greed is a generous heart. The only way out of our maelstrom of misery is to be magnanimous. The generous men among us demonstrate that we gain our lives by giving them away. They show us that in the end we possess nothing except what we have shared.

As Ron confessed at a men's overnight:

> *"At mid-life I have figured out that life is primarily a matter of giving rather than getting. Giving of myself*

to that which is larger, longer, lovelier than my own individual being. Giving is no secondary or superfluous activity. It is the highest act I will ever perform. I am made rich by my generosity."

X *We want* TO OPEN UP THE TEARDUCTS

"Tears wash the cobwebs from your attic."

Spanish proverb

We humans don't cry very well, particularly in America, especially men. Studies show that normal men vary from zero to seven crying episodes per month and zero to twenty-nine for women. Even when men cry, our tears are more controlled. We well up, but seldom flow, rarely sob.

In fear of being called whiny, wimpish little boys, we "tough it out" and pay dearly for that practice. As one physician aptly notes: "Sorrows which find no vent in tears may soon make other organs weep." My hunch is that many men are walking around with other organs weeping inappropriately because

24

we have paid insufficient heed to crying with our eyes, throats, and hearts.

But the new male is beginning, slowly but surely, to be emotionally expressive—to open up the tearducts in order to cleanse the system of poisons and to restore physical and spiritual balance.

You see male politicians crying. Humphrey, Muskie, and others have set the tone in recent times.

You see male athletes crying in moments of agony and ecstasy.

You see husbands dissolving in tears when abandoned by wives, and fathers no longer displaying stiff upper lips when offspring set out on their own.

Today we see new men observing the 11th commandment: "Thou shalt be brave, open, and moved enough to weep anytime of the day or night during thy stay on this planet."

There is good biblical backing for men's crying. In that torturous tale of intrigue, betrayal, and forgiveness among Joseph and his brothers, near the end, Joseph is overcome with feelings of fondness for his kin, and he weeps not once, twice, or three times, but on six separate occasions.

In the New Testament, we come across the following verse: "And Jesus wept." It may be the shortest verse in the Bible, but, a mighty phrase. Jesus was distraught over the rotten behavior in Jerusalem, and instead of ranting and railing, instead of drafting an oration or mounting a demonstration, he was moved to tears. He wept.

Sometimes falling to pieces is the way we make our point and put ourselves back together again.

The ancient Hebrews, my friend relates, kept two tear cups on the mantel in their homes—one for sad tears, the other for happy ones. A case can be made for more cups: for tears of anger, tears of hope, tears of laughter.

If the point of existence is to be sufficiently moved by joy, sorrow, anger, or hope to be able to move others, then tears are a prime indicator of our being alive.

Men would be well served by having tear cups handy.

XI *We want* TO SALUTE THE WILDMAN

Inside each of us is raw male energy which sets us to growling. Feminists have called this "the beast within" when describing a similar force within themselves.

Some men are raging beasts within; they live out of control. They resemble Rambo on a rampage.

But new males, sensitive almost to a fault, hunger to reclaim and release what poet Robert Bly calls our "wildman" in order to achieve balance. We are learning to roar as well as cry on the path to fuller manhood.

As Raul said in a men's workshop: "When I grunt and growl, it cuts the edge off my destructive impulses."

Terry exclaimed:

"I am learning to engage in physical competition without beating the other guy's brains out. Someday I hope to be able to wrestle men in a playful manner."

Two years ago my wife, Carolyn, and I, with another couple, were riding a zodiac raft along the tumultuous NaPali coast in Hawaii. Bouncing, hanging on for dear life, I let out belly-deep yells of fear, abandon, and exhilaration. In those moments I felt close to the wildman within myself.

Another example: I admire, and occasionally try to emulate, the ancient Druids who built gigantic bonfires and gathered around them dancing and screaming wildly to scare away demons. This makes more humane sense to me than sacrificing goats, hanging witches, or tearing up neighborhoods on Halloween.

New men are walking a fine yet crucial line between being wild and being savage.

XII *We want*
TO FIND A CALLING

"You can't eat for eight hours a day nor drink for eight hours a day nor make love for eight hours a day—all you can do for eight hours is work. Which is probably the reason why we make ourselves and everybody else so miserable and unhappy."

William Faulkner

We men hunger for more than jobs; we seek professions: positions where we can profess our views, share our hearts, be more of who we are.

In seminars on "Finding Your Calling," I ask men to wrestle with fundamental questions whether they are in their teens or near retirement age.

29

First, what do I really want to do with the rest of my life? The past is the past. Before asking what the marketplace looks like, or how much money I need, or what is my training...the bedrock question is: How do I wish to invest my remaining moments on this planet?

Another way to ask it: What is my vocation—what invokes, evokes, provokes the deepest gifts of my being?

I know plenty of men who have quit jobs they loathe to pursue professions that summon their creativity and stretch their capacities.

Second, what do I like to do when no one else is telling me what to do? This playful question can uncover passions that energize our leisure moments. We men need to pay attention to our hobbies, because some of our avocations might prove large enough in meaning to become vocations.

Third, I ask men: whom are you trying to please in your life-work? Your father, your grandmother, your junior high teacher? There is nothing wrong with pleasing any or all of these folks. Yet you and I will travel to our graves alone and must also please ourselves as well as others. Our work *and* our values must mesh for us to be whole men.

Fourth, I ask them to consider a helpful tip I once received from a colleague: "Don't use your work to get love. Work to get cash, even garner meaning, but love cannot be earned, only given and received."

He was reminding us not to expect jobs to fill our love needs. Love happens with friends and family. We men need to remember that we are "lovable" before we ever show up at work and long after we go home.

Our goal as men is to find fulfilling work. When we are fortunate to locate our true calling, and then to do it, our days taste good, exceptionally good.

XIII *We want*
TO OWN OUR MISTAKES

"All life is an experiment. The more experiments you make the better. What if you are a little coarse, and you get your coat soiled or torn. What if you do fall and get fairly rolled in the dirt once or twice? Up again, never be so afraid of a tumble."

Ralph Waldo Emerson

Men are driven, even damaged, by trying to be perfectionists. We are terror-stricken at the prospect of being failures.

In counseling, Timothy broke down and cried:

> *"As a youngster, being afraid of failure, I hid out. I acted above it all. Only now at twenty-nine have I realized that nothing ventured,*

nothing grown. I don't have a great job. My relationships with women are fair. I haven't got a close male friend. But since I have been risking some, I am growing up. Watch out—I'm on my way!"

Charlie Brown is eating a peanut butter and jelly sandwich. He looks admiringly at his hands and says: "Hands are fascinating things. I like my hands. I think I have nice hands. My hands seem to have a lot of character. These are hands which may someday accomplish great things. These are hands which may someday do marvelous works!"

He is going strong by now. "They may build mighty bridges or heal the sick or hit home-runs or write soul-stirring novels!" Charlie is yelling.

"These are hands which may someday change the course of destiny!" Lucy looks down at Charlie's hands and says, "They've got jelly on them!"

Lucy is painfully perceptive, but we Charlie Browns are not so easily derailed. Our hands do have jelly on them. They are messy and flawed, but they are *our* hands. We still use them to produce fresh, marvelous creations throughout our lifetimes.

33

New men recognize that we can fail without being failures. We can fall down and rise again. Like accomplished jazz musicians, we can make our mistakes mean something.

Lick your fingers clean, Charlie Brown; destiny needs a hand. Yours!

XIV *We want*
TO JOIN MEN'S GROUPS

"I'm a self-made man, but I think if I had it to do over again, I'd call in others."

Roland Young

Men are doing more together nowadays than sitting around playing cards, watching football, and drinking beer. One of America's burgeoning revolutions finds men meeting to share pieces of their deep hopes and hurts. The new male is tired of being stolid and self-sufficient. He longs to exchange touch and thought with brothers.

Charles, a friend of mine, who is a prominent, relentless advocate for men's rights and growth, told me recently:

35

*"We men have related to one another in two primary ways: (1) **Side-by-side** as work associates, committee members, and team players; or (2) **Back-to-back** as cohorts in the military or police force where we cover for each other in life-dependent situations.*

*Now we are finally learning to enjoy **face-to-face** encounters where we talk directly to one another as brothers in close, personal, trusting fashion."*

The inactive male says: "No problem. I am fine as I am." The reactive man says: "I'll take may cues from women." The pro-active man offers: "I have a need to be liberated by myself, for myself—first and foremost. My primary gift to women, other men, and children is a self freed from the masculinity traps (subtle and overt) to which I have been enslaved. We adult males have found the adversary, and he is us. Women serve as accomplices in crime, but we are our own worst enemies. I plan to do something about my condition. I will start by relating to men, face-to-face."

The Men's Movement will wither if our main motivation is backlash against

36

the Women's Movement or if our primary goal, as one person put it, is "to provide childcare at feminist events and do typing for feminist publications," as important as these efforts are.

We must identify with and immerse ourselves in the singular pain, pride, power, and pleasure associated with being new men in the 1980's and 90's. We must become "at cause" rather than remain "at effect." After all, no one knows what it is really like to be men but us men.

We are each our own expert, but we join a larger movement of men to exchange notes, to hold and shove one another, to create tomorrows together. There aren't any Santa Clauses or theories or women or children or religions to account for what we do with who we are. We're responsible for ourselves.

There are many reasons, as women have long realized, for gender-based dialogues. First, there are male concerns that are properly and beneficially shared man to man—for example, fathering and being fathered.

Mixed company tends to distract men from facing the necessary challenges, comraderie, and comfort for growing our selves. As psychologist Sam

Keen notes: "There is much about our experience as men that can only be shared with and understood by other men."

Second, there is considerable healing to be achieved between men because we have been pounding upon, even destroying one another, ever since Cain slew his brother Abel. We need to learn respectful, loving ways to be brothers, not to be our brother's boss, keeper, or lackey, but our brother's brother.

Often we men build bonds with each other only to run into deeply ingrained homophobia about intimacy. As Lloyd lamented: "I get close to men, then I back off; I move toward them, then move away. It's a frustrating, crazy dance." Or we men feel comfortable being open and intimate with our buddies during a men's group, but revert to negative, distancing patterns when back at work amid the "good old boy's network."

We have a long way to go in the process of joining with one another. New men are learning to feel clear and comfortable as they grow closer to their brothers.

The best way for us to heal our brother wounds and befriend our brother fears is to spend time sharing aches and aspirations, telling our real stories, face-to-face, brother to brother, as peers in supportive, open places.

Sometimes women are jealous or uneasy about what happens in men's groups. Occasionally a female companion feels that her place as best friend is eroded by her partner's buddies.

In twenty years of participation in the Men's Movement I have observed the opposite result: building bonds with men usually strengthens and deepens a man's primary connection with his female mate.

Bert put it this way to his wife, Gail:

"I choose to be with male friends not to supplant but to supplement our love. Gail, I need you to trust that I don't turn to men to fill your gaps but to enjoy the unique gifts of their friendship.

As you need female confidantes, so I covet male buddies. Close friends have proven to be one of my most nourishing finds during our twelve years of marriage.

Believe me, I will never do anything with another man or woman which will injure or jeopardize our partnership."

39

XV *We want*
TO ENTER DEEP SOLITUDE

"It is in deep solitude that I find the gentleness with which I can truly love others. It is pure affection and filled with reverence for the solitude of others."

Thomas Merton

Thomas Merton was a Trappist monk who lived much of his life as a hermit, but whose solitude led him into close, caring communion with other human beings. It's the rhythm that counts. The art of a full life is to juggle sufficient times for action and reflection, engagement and withdrawal. Merton and other spiritual giants have accomplished this balancing act.

The end of one of Albert Camus' short stories raises the question whether a word written in small letters on an artist's canvas should be read as solitary or solidary. Sensitive, growing men embrace both moments of solitariness and solidarity in order to lead complete lives.

New men live people-focused lives, *and* we intentionally carve out times for renewal. I think of Hosea's invitation in the Old Testament: "I will entice you into the desert, and there I will speak to you in the depths of your heart."

Most of us don't live near deserts, or if we do, we don't go there on a regular basis. The new male seeks equivalent places of serenity and silence where he can reflect undisturbed, engage in creative brooding, converse with his God.

In medieval times, homes were blessed with meditation areas or rooms for quiet. Today, sacred spaces are hard to come by. We might consider retreating to our attics to find a place for calming our souls. I know of men who are creating private corners, here or there, for "holy time."

Antoine de St. Exupéry once raised a fruitful question for the male spiritual quest: "What are we worth when motionless?" It is difficult for men to feel valuable unless we are achieving something, on the move, productive. We are slow to appreciate our worth when silent, solitary, still.

Community and aloneness, involvement and contemplation: open, expansive, new men seek all of these.

XVI *We want*
TO BECOME JUGGLERS

Our family is fortunate to live near Balboa Park in San Diego which holds a veritable carnival of delights on the weekends. I am especially mesmerized by jugglers whose daring and agility keep everything imaginable up in the air. I am a juggler of sorts, too. There are five major priorities (in no particular order) that I juggle daily: personhood, partnership, parenting, ministry, and planetary citizenship. Then there are all the sub-concerns of each. You can imagine the air traffic in my sky.

I love jugglers not only because I identify with them, but also because they have so much to teach me as an adult male.

First, through patient practice most jugglers have honed their skill to a consummate state. You don't see jugglers sharing their wares in the park until they've done ample homework. Good jugglers don't wing it with swords and torches until they are ready.

Second, jugglers aren't perfect. Like us all, they occasionally drop a ball, even several of them, yet the show goes on, covered by timely patter and a forgiving crowd. A perfect juggler would drive us crazy and right out of the park.

Third, juggling is play and reminds us goal-oriented, intense types to ply our trade seriously but not grimly. Just like our jobs, juggling families or private lives can be all-absorbing; while everything is up in the air you hardly think about much else, yet down deep, at core, it remains a playful act.

That's the main lesson for me, and it's the one I want to pass on to my brothers: keep your sense of the lighthearted even as you juggle heavy life-and-death stuff. Remember you are a re-creational being.

Men are playful animals by nature; we forget that truth at great peril to our manhood and to our globe.

XVII   WE WANT TO BE MORE THAN A "MAN MOM"!

"Delight in your children openly. Give yourself, your humor, your small talk, and the minor affections of your hands and eyes. They aren't going to see many people who care. . .it would be nice if their father could be one."

Robert Capon

I read an article in *The New Yorker* that depicted fathers as "blocks of marble, giant cubes, highly polished, with veins and seams—placed squarely in the path of children. Fathers cannot be climbed over, neither can they be slithered past." I find the image reactionary, inaccurate, and derogatory.

Margaret Mead claimed that fatherhood is a "social invention learned

45

somewhere at the dawn of history. The role of father is a psychologically foreign one artificially imposed by the culture for the survival of the race."

Wait a minute, Margaret, cries the new male trying valiantly to be a full-fledged father! A woman, despite her fundamental biological connection with a child, isn't automatically a mother with all the subtleties and complexities that word implies. Fathers and mothers must both be essentially trained for their child-rearing functions. We both have to learn how to be kind and loving and how to want and care for a child.

Children unwittingly mouth distorted sentiments, too. In a paperback entitled *To Dad*, one child says "A Dad is a man mom!" The rest of the descriptions are just as cute and just as disheartening.

However, it's not up to partners, poets, social scientists, children, or cartoonists to alter radically our perception and appreciation of fathering. It is primarily up to fathers who believe our position is being minimized, misrepresented, even maligned, and who want to demonstrate to ourselves, our children, and our world the true stature and place of fatherhood.

New males are not interested in

settling for second-class citizenship as fathers. They are interested in reducing the mother-chauvinism rampant in our culture by displaying fresh attitudes and behaviors. Their stories and struggles inspire other men to join their ranks.

Bob told our retreat on fathering:

"I wasn't always a father, but when I became one, I signed a contract for life. I once was a free spirit who could ride off on a horse in most any direction or tell most any situation to go to hell. Not anymore. There is no running away from Mark and Amy. Being a father is being a physical, emotional, social, and spiritual presence, from here on out."

Alvin has this growing perspective on his fathering:

"That's the way it is with my children. We love one another in different ways and not always the ways we would choose to be loved but the ways we are able to love. Our bond is limited and unfinished yet real and deep. There is nothing more important in my life than being a father to Chuck and Susan."

Edward reflected on his place as a father:

"As fathers we are prone to extremes: either we feel successful if our children turn out well or failures if they flop. I am learning to quit giving myself so much credit or blame and start giving most of both to my children."

James pondered being a stepfather:

"My children did not select me. They simply inherited me when I married their mother. I always respect the fact that they never got the chance to say anything about the disruption, then restructuring, of their family. It keeps me humble, honest, awake."

I personally believe that we parents don't *raise* children at all; we *relate* to them. We raise flags, blinds, arms, and corn but not other humans. We foster an environment, but children grow themselves. We are catalysts and providers, but we are not the determiners of our children's lives.

So I try to parent essentially from and for myself. There is profound relationship and ongoing feedback, but I

48

act on the basis of what feels right to me as a father in response to four irrepeatable children.

This means if I want to hug our sons or daughters, then I give it rather than beg or barter for it. I have found the following epigram to hold true for my fathering: give and ye shall often receive; wait to receive and ye shall often resent.

It is a delight when our children respond to our clumsy, heartfelt gestures of love. It is a thrill when they reciprocate or initiate their own affection.

Charlie Brown states in the Peanuts cartoon:

> *"My Dad likes to have me come down to the barber shop and wait for him. No matter how busy he is, even if the shop is full of customers, he always stops to say 'hi' to me. I sit here on the bench until six o'clock, when he's through, and then we ride home together. IT REALLY DOESN'T TAKE MUCH TO MAKE A DAD HAPPY___"*

You're damn right, Charlie Brown.

49

XVIII *We want*
TO REMOVE OUR MASKS

*"When a man's self is hidden from every-
body else . . . it seems also to become
hidden even from himself, and it permits
disease and death to gnaw into his
substance without his clear knowledge."*

Sidney Jourard

Men are emerging from hiding of all
kinds. There is pain in self-disclosure.
There is loss in becoming more
transparent. As Andre Berthiaume says:
"We all wear masks, and the time comes
when we cannot remove them without
removing some of our own skin." As
difficult and hurtful as the process is, the
rewards for shedding our masks are
worth it.

I am aware of brothers who are
willing to remove their masks and find

50

new meaning.

Curt said: "I have found a deeper meaning in Jesus's words: 'Let down your nets.' In letting down my guard, my defenses, I am opening up myself and will never close as tightly again. It's scary, but the results are promising."

Michael told our support group: "Frankly, the more emotionally constipated I am, the lousier I feel about myself. In this safe, supportive group I am beginning to reveal parts of myself that have been hidden for years."

Julius said: "I am hungry for emotional intimacy with other men. I have put all my relational eggs in a basket with women. I desperately need to diversify. Even the Lone Ranger had a male companion, Tonto, before whom he must have taken off his mask once in a while and unveiled his soft, hurting, warm sides."

I have always been fascinated by one of the first things out of God's mouth in the Old Testament. It was a probing question to Adam and Eve in the garden: "Where are you?" (Genesis 3: 9). This was not so much a query of geography as it was one of morality.

Where are we in relationship to one another? Where are we in relationship to our purpose on earth? Where are we in relationship to animals? Where are we in relationship to our creator?

From the beginnings of human history we have been asked to come out from hiding into the open, toward greater self-disclosure.

Being ultra-mask-uline is not a healthy choice for new men.

XIX   *We want*
TO TAKE BETTER CARE
OF OURSELVES

I am haunted by Mickey Mantle's remark to a sportswriter some years after he retired. The former New York Yankee baseball star stated: "If I knew I was going to live this long, I would have taken better care of myself."

Droves of American men are exercising, jogging, and working out at gyms and health spas. We should be in better shape than our fathers were, and we are. But, bigger and better-toned muscles to the contrary, American males still live an average of eight years (ten for children born today) less than our female counterparts. Three times as many men as women fall prey to cardiovascular—renal diseases related to stress,

53

overwork, and worry.

Furthermore, in 1900 the incidence of stomach ulcers was primarily among women, but today men have three to four times as many ulcers as women—another disease indicative of psychological pressure.

Men have a 300 to 400 percent greater chance of dying through homicide or suicide than do women. Our cancer rate tops that of women by 40 percent. Men are prone to leukemia. Men begin to have hardening of the arteries in their early twenties, while it is virtually absent in women until they have passed forty.

A few more emotional ailments for painful measure. We males are three times more susceptible to obsessive-compulsive neurosis, and five to ten times more likely to become psychopathic personalities than women.

The simple truth is that "machismo kills."

These facts are encouraging men to alter their work, nutritional, and exercise habits. The new male knows his health is in trouble unless he transforms his daily routines from self-abusive to self-affirming ones.

Jerry remarks that being in a stress management program sponsored by his company has helped to turn his life inside out. "I know that I can't conquer the stress in my life, but I can manage it better now."

Max takes midday walks to a nearby park and sits quietly there by himself. . .empty of pressures.

Joe knows that unless he builds tennis matches into the flow of his week, frustrations accumulate, then he explodes.

Merle put it this way:

"After my parents died, I realized that I needed to take charge of my own health, my own life, and stop banking on parents to rescue me. This shift in attitude was what I needed to make changes in my behavior. I'm on my way to a healthier second half of life now."

One way to reduce stress is to experience the rejuvenation that flowers from being a giver. Recent surveys show that giving people live healthier and longer lives.

Eminent psychiatrist Karl Menninger told his patients that giving generously of

55

their talents, time, and resources to causes outside themselves would combat physical illness and promote emotional well-being.

A Yale study of men in mid-life declares that those involved in social organizations, contributing beyond their work lives, and sharing emotional closeness live fuller and longer lives than men who keep to themselves.

Taking better care of ourselves *and* taking better care of those around us are linked, reinforcing pursuits which new men blend.

56

XX *We want*
TO LEARN EARTHLINESS

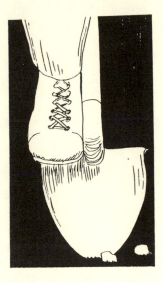

"We need to learn earthliness, and serve its ends, to feel its hands about us like a friend."

Rainer Maria Rilke

We men have made our living, gained our positions as managers of the natural world through unbridled technology. The results have often been devastating. Our web of life—the air, water, soil, food, and even rain—are poisoned by industrial waste and invaded by deadly radiation.

Mountains, deserts, and plains have been raped of their treasures.

57

Fellow creatures—plants, animals, birds, and fish—have been robbed of their natural habitats. New species disappear each year.

The ecological havoc wreaked by our hands gives us pause. Men today feel an urgent ethical imperative to repent, turn around, and amend our ways from exploiters to caretakers, hoping it's not too late.

The new male holds the organic view that we are part of an interdependent web, and if any part is broken or torn, the whole shudders.

The new male acknowledges, not just intellectually but viscerally, that we humans are related to and a product of nature. There is a ground-floor kinship between us and all other living beings.

I am jarred to recall the chiding of the Hopi: "When you American men say you *under*stand, you really mean *over*stand." I am haunted by the words of an old holy Wintu women who cried out: "How can the spirit of the earth like the white man? Everywhere the white man has touched it, it is sore."

In these years of our planet's need, even if we men stop our intentional plundering, we will most likely never put to rest our unintentional blundering, even the most alert among us. Our spaceship is fragile. So are we, its caretakers.

Instead of quitting or pointing fingers at one another, let us use the simple tools at our human disposal. The tools of economics, of science, of politics, and especially the tools born of the religious spirit.

We men can give no greater gift to those who carry on after us than to handle our greetings with earth with exceeding care and tenderness.

XXI *We want* TO HAVE MEN-TORS

"The mentor represents a mixture of parent and peer; they must be both and not purely either one."

Daniel Levinson

The Latin word *mentor* means "wise one" or "counselor." In Greek mythology, Mentor was a valued peer, an advisor to Odysseus, than a guide to Telemachus, Odysseus's son.

Men benefit from the example, nudging, and comfort not only of our fathers, brothers, and buddies, but also of mentors—those individuals who can teach us skills and awareness essential to the process of growing up. Mentors help us in ways those at home cannot. They don't replace parental figures but rather supplement them and other loved ones.

60

They are older than our peers and often younger than our fathers. They come and go, helping us through transitions.

When men are asked to identify their mentors, they often well up with tears, recalling those who have played critical, life-affirming roles in their journeys.

I think of several in my own history: Walt, who reminded me to have fun while remaining serious; Ted and Andy, whose way with words still provides a model for my own speaking; Frank, whose smile lingers in my mind's eye; John, who wisely pushed me into difficult territory when I didn't appear ready to travel there; Roy, who showed me quiet, gentle power as a leader; Anthony, who evoked the teamwork *and* the competitive side of my nature.

Think of the men-tors who have helped mold your character...remember them with a call, a note, a prayer.

XXII *We want*
TO QUIT BREAST-BEATING

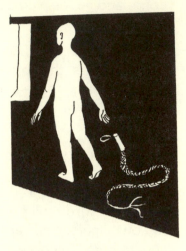

Let's give up the pernicious habit of self-flagellation, not only for Lent, but forever.

In counseling and group discussions with men, I hear more breast-beating nowadays. Over the years men have taken out our frustrations on women, children, and animals. But pounding ourselves is becoming an all too common exercise. It is a dead-end practice.

Self-flagellation occurs whenever a person abuses him or herself unnecessarily and regularly. The forms are subtle and varied.

Hal blames himself for the fact that his daughter made a second shaky engagement and his son dropped out of college.

Rick is addicted to female barbs, taking every potshot to heart.

Leonard takes personally every catastrophe in the business he manages. His ulcers are the sorry result. Listen to this cartoon which depicts the consequence of self-flagellation:

> *"When I was a kid I had the fire of creation in my belly.*
>
> *Fortunately, I was practical enough to see that it gets you nowhere!*
>
> *I'm forty-five now, and I've got it made, except for this fire in my belly!*
>
> *The doctor says: 'It's an ulcer!' "*

To become fulfilled men we must practice the distinction between self-criticism and self-flagellation.

We won't long survive on self-pity and neurotic remorse. Guilt and blame are cheap emotional responses we use to avoid right action and creative companionship.

We men aren't only "bad boys, inadequate husbands, hopeless sexists, and lousy fathers." We must salute our existent and potential beauty, if we are to make essential changes and move toward our visions.

Self-flagellation is an insidious addiction to be given up by grown men.

XXIII *We want*
TO COMPLETE
NOT ONLY COMPETE

"Behold, how good and pleasant it is when brothers dwell together in unity!"

Psalm 133:1

As boys we grow up competing and never quite kick the habit. We vie against one another in sports and schoolwork. We are taught to pursue victory, often at all costs. We compete against women and men, then later, with our own children.

Years back I remember a struggle where as a parent I competed *through* our son. It was the Cub Scouts' Pinewood Derby competition. On the surface, it was a seemingly harmless, fun-filled scouting activity for our sons. Russ and I participated in our first Pinewood competition when he was seven and I was thirty-four, back in Iowa. On the whole, the cub scouts came out of it emotionally unscathed. I'm not sure that some of us fathers fared as well.

The rumors were heavy that the fathers were the real competitors and that the boys were merely fronts for the skills, imaginations, and drives of the parents. Anxieties invaded my heart: I had no woodworking tools, and I was inept at building things. Yet my ego wanted Russ to perform well his first time out.

I didn't want our son to flunk on the basis of my inability and lack of equipment. Consequently, I summoned the talent of a craftsman named Otto, a friend in our congregation, and the three of us (mainly Otto) built a powerhouse little racer called the "Golden Gopher," #65. Russ won second place in the entire pack for speed. Russ won! Russ won?

As cubmaster, I had a voice in planning the second year. For the first time ever, I encouraged our pack to give out awards to every boy who participated: not just entrance ribbons but actual awards for the sleekest, the meanest looking, the bluest, the weirdest, and so forth. We were making up categories as swiftly as we could look over the entries.

It sounded like a good, fair idea, except that the other fathers pushed to give special trophies to the three fastest cars. Three boys still got fancier awards than the others. Furthermore, I'm not sure many of the youngsters were really fooled, let alone pleased, by this new strategy.

The third year I was going to hold out for every boy receiving equivalent awards, but the council of planners overruled me saying: "Isn't that tantamount to calling the whole thing off? What happened to good old-fashioned competition?"

Fortunately, we left town before the next Pinewood Derby.

I am not asking us to abandon competition altogether, whether at work or play. But let's not be governed by it. Vince Lombardi misstated when he said: "Winning isn't everything. It's the only thing." New men do not have to triumph in order to enjoy themselves. We can lose sometimes and still be winners.

There are men who exemplify this emerging attitude toward play and competition.

Samuel told our Saturday seminar:

"For me, winning isn't everything; it isn't the only thing. It is simply one thing among many others. When it is missing I can usually have a good, productive time playing, whereas its presence in no way insures an enjoyable experience."

Johnny tells us:

*"I'm less interested in **beating** my opponents than in **meeting** my own personal standards for achievement, enjoyment, and growth. The sound of cheering within is what I hunger for."*

I recently read in a Runner's Magazine a male long-distance runner's comment: "I have only one goal left—not to break my personal records or race some distance or place I've never gone before. My goal now is simply to become an old runner."

Reflect on the story of Mark Spitz, the 1972 Olympic Gold medalist, seven times over. When he crawled out of the water after earning his last gold medal, he said he never wanted to swim again. Swimming wasn't worth it to him; he wasn't having fun. Americans lost connection with this outstanding competitor. We turned him off, because we want to swim for the fun of it.

At men's gatherings we participate in group games like horseshoes and volleyball. We keep score, but we also participate in new games like earth ball, yogi tag, frisbee—imaginative play flowing from cooperation more than competition. We are learning to play fair, play hard, and play for the sake of playfulness.

As the Psalmist wrote: "How good and pleasant it is when brothers dwell together in unity...," not locked in combat or competition but in closeness and cooperation where our gifts complement rather than undercut those of our brothers.

New men yearn to share games and activities of completion: swapping our various skills and truths, becoming whole individuals within the whole human family.

XXIV *We want*
TO SIMPLIFY

"Simplicity, simplicity, simplicity!
I say, let your affairs be as two or
three, and not a hundred or a thousand . . .
Simplify, simplify."

Henry David Thoreau

Men are engaged in shedding
pounds, yet the art of shedding
expectations, objects, and illusions is not
so easy.

Arnold Bennett, author of *How to
Live on Twenty-Four Hours a Day,* was
once confronted by a man who showered
compliments on the book saying: "And
now, thanks to you and your book, I am
going to concentrate." Asked Bennett,
"On what?" "Oh," said the man, "on lots
and lots of things!"

Men are recognizing that it is time to *forget* lots and lots of things, and to focus on a few primary efforts in our lives, to find our special themes. Greed is a common male malaise, described as chasing two hares at the same time, thereby having both escape one's grasp.

Sam Levenson remarked that when he was a boy he used to have to do what his father wanted, and now he has to do what his children want. When can he do what he wants? Well, at some time in our adult male lives, usually around midlife, we begin to accept and live out our bedrock life-theme rather than avoid it.

In workshops on "Shedding" I invite men to let go of the superfluous and zero in on fundamental hungers.

First, I ask them to go into their attics, offices, garages, and closets to throw or give "stuff" away. A yard sale every few years is a way of shedding things rather than forcing our children to dispose of our belongings when we die.

Some men are packrats, but an abundance of objects doesn't prove our worthiness as persons. Our truly important material possessions can usually be transported in a suitcase. In my case, a few books, stamps, sheet music, and photo albums are all I personally need.

Second, I ask men to do psychic cleansing, to let go of nagging frustrations and nibbling guilts burdening our lives. We get clear about our priorities in order to create trimmer, more authentic tomorrows.

Altogether too much energy and effort is spent upon impossibilities or low priorities. We men can't have everything, do everything, achieve whatever we want. The challenge is to be energetic about possibilities in our lives.

Graduates of these "Shedding" workshops make considerable progress in simplifying their lives.

Jed told us: "I now travel more lightly and simply as I come around the bend, more purposefully too, since I unloaded material and spiritual baggage that had been weighing me down."

Carlos said: "Every day I try to feed my body with good food and exercise, my mind with wisdom, my spirit with rest, my heart with laughter, and my conscience with worthy deeds. When I do that, my diet is balanced."

Roger announced to the group at the close of the weekend: "I plan *beyond* the present, but I can only live *in* the present. I will no longer postpone what I believe to be true, beautiful, and loving until tomorrow. I'm going to quit saving my life and start spending it."

New men honor our complexity when we choose to simplify our lives.

XXV   *We want*
TO HAVE A "SPIRITUAL"

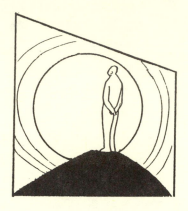

"The purpose of life is simply to grow a soul."

A. Powell Davies

We men go in for physicals regularly. How often do we have a "spiritual?" Have we ever had our souls checked, x-rayed, tuned, overhauled?

The major male complaint—being out of breath and bushed—mandates a spiritual cure. We need to be re-inspired.

I have been active in the Men's Movement since its early stages. My involvement started in the Los Angeles area around 1972. I have seen the movement develop from a reactive to a proactive experience for men, from one concerned initially with the impact of women's liberation upon men, to its current focus on male rights, risks, and responsibilities.

I have been a participant and leader in men's support and discussion groups, retreats and action projects, gay-straight encounters—the gamut of men's emphases and evolution.

One largely unexplored region in the movement remains: spirituality. We have addressed money, sexuality, parenting and being parented, law, relationships, ecology, work, commitment, death— most everything except the demands and comforts, difficulties and benefits of the spiritual quest.

I have come to believe that our male malaise is a spiritual one at root. We have our physical agonies and emotional immaturities, but, deep down, our fundamental struggle is spiritual. We hanker to find more meaning, profounder fulfillment, a durable, lasting peace within and without our lives.

Sam Keen certainly depicts modern American men when he challenges us with these words:

"I think religions and therapies might be defined by the way they answer the question: What are we to do

75

*about the yearning, the emptiness,
the hunger, the nothingness that
huddle close to the core of human
experience? What are we to do with
the embarrassing awareness of the
incompleteness of life? I think we
create the problem when we define
the nostalgia for completeness as
abnormal or wrong. We are
ashamed of our metaphysical
hungers."*

Yes, Sam, my brothers and I are too
often ashamed to confess our
metaphysical hungers, and we rarely
strive to feed them.

"What does it profit us, "says the
New Testament, "if we gain the whole
world and forfeit our very souls?" When
men face up to our frantic foolishness,
we know only too well that gaining the
whole world at the price of losing our
very souls is a lousy deal.

But I'm not cynical, self-pitying, or
despairing. I experience hope in the
current, valiant attempts of new men to
make peace with their beings.

Harry told our men's meditation
class that it provided him an opportunity
to stop thinking and talking compulsively.
Spiritual discipline was a place to cease
the incessant clatter in his skull and to

76

listen to the subtler, oft-soothing sounds of his interior.

Clancy's meditation enables him to feel a mystical kinship with the cosmos of which he is an integral, breathing part.

Martin works from dawn to dusk, but he finds time every day to contemplate. He knows mere moments of "centering" are an economical and effective way to handle the pressures of his work.

Howard cites some of the physical and emotional benefits of regular spiritual exercise. He is relaxed, needs less sleep, and his senses are heightened. Colors are vivid, and music sounds richer.

As one colleague states: "We do not gain time for living as a result of spiritual discipline, but we live more, because our senses are alive and open to the world around us."

Stephen found he was peaceful *and* awake after his short, spiritual breaks.

The religious imperative for men is to balance the inner and the outer life, to blend images of knight and hermit. Men like Buddha and Jesus were contemplatives and prophets. They didn't employ spiritual exercise as a moral cop-out. The Tao says that "a sound person's heart dare not be shut up within itself."

Many spiritual leaders have traveled to the mountain top, then returned, refreshed and ready to serve people in the valleys below. They were not escapists.

The great ones believe that their spirituality is never complete until someone else feels more loved by them. The spiritual life enables us to contribute breath and meaning to the universe that created us.

XXVI   *We want*
TO CLIMB OFF THE LADDER

"There are two tragedies to life. One is not to get your heart's desire. The other is to get it."

George Bernard Shaw

My brother is a psychotherapist who, in midlife, has written songs to underscore the messages of his counseling. One song warns fellow men to cease climbing up and over one another.

Here are some of the lyrics he put to a pop-rock melody.

"Talked with a man the other day. I was going up, he was going down. He said, 'Before it's too late, turn yourself around on the ladder.'

Climbing up the ladder, climbing up

*the ladder to success. Stepping on
some hands, stepping on some toes.
It comes with the territory,
everybody knows.*

*Buck it up, suck it up, aiming for the
top, no time to change your mind,
you can't get off. Can't stop runnin',
got to catch the guy ahead. No
place for feeling, no room for regret,
scare him down, wear him down.*

*Climbing up the ladder, up the
ladder, ladder, ladder... I can't stop
until I reach the top of the ladder,
the ladder..."*

The song continues in frenzied
fashion and ends with a loud, crashing
thud!

American men are obsessed with
conquering heights, reaching pinnacles,
standing on platforms. Pulpits, as the
quip goes, allow preachers (still mostly
men) to pontificate from "six feet above
contradiction." We men can be far too
lofty, remote, and isolated from the rest
of humanity.

The new male is emerging. He
shouts: "Let me down; it's too lonely up
here at the top!" Men suffering from what
has been aptly labelled "success
depression" resonate with Shaw's

statement that we can be done in by ambition, by reaching "our heart's desire."

In the Old Testament, Genesis 28:12, the author tells us that Jacob "dreamed that there was a ladder set up on the earth, and the top of it reached to heaven; and behold, the angels of God were ascending and descending on it!" The truth is that descending is as important a movement in life as ascending.

At the very moment in history when women are practicing assertiveness, men are hungering for more relaxation. Women are climbing corporate and other ladders and men, sometimes squawkingly, other times with great relief, are descending several notches or getting off the ladder altogether.

Sometimes being still is the best way to go on.

Years ago, the President of a prestigious eastern college used his sabbatical to work at blue-collar, odd jobs for six months in order to broaden and deepen his life experience. Since college, Herb had lived entirely in "ivory towers." He wanted down.

The sabbatical experience made him a far more sympathetic, less driven, college President when he returned to campus. He was able to relate more meaningfully to students and faculty as well as to his own family.

His ambition was balanced with a new sense of humility. He began to embody the quality that philosopher Walter Kauffmann called "humbition": an appropriate blend of innocence and cunning.

XXVII *We want*
TO DISCOVER
OUR TRUE SELVES

"Each of us has an undiscovered continent of self. May we become Columbuses of our souls."

Goethe

In a world systematically trying to deny us self-possession, being who we truly are is one of the noblest journeys we humans ever navigate.

The contemporary male identity is shaky and unclear, up for grabs. We are encouraged to be sensitive, but often when we are, females exclaim: "Hey, act like a man!" We men want to be gentle without being labelled "wimpish." We try to be strong without being called "macho."

We are beginning to practice equality with women at about the same time they are trying autonomy and independence on for size. As poet Ric Masten laments:

> *"I have noticed*
> *that men*
> *somewhere around forty*
> *tend to come in from the field*
> *with a sigh*
> *and removing their coat in the hall*
> *call into the kitchen*
> > *you were right*
> > *grace*
> > *it ain't out there*
> > *just like you've always said*
> *and she*
> *with the children gone at last*
> *breathless*
> *puts her hat on her head*
> > *the hell it ain't*
> *coming and going*
> *they pass*
> *in the doorway."*

Let's use this strategy in our lifelong quest to locate, then fulfill, our "manhood." Write down a list of our expectations from primary people in our lives: parents, work associates, companions, and children. Then cross off, one by one, any *external*

84

expectations that don't correspond with our *internal* aspirations.

Many men lug around extraneous, irrelevant baggage even though it doesn't belong to us anymore. We need to clean house.

I have met new men who have possession of their own existence. Sid said: "It is time to be the best me. Other versions of me haven't matched up with the special being I want to be."

Andy stated: "Now, at thirty-four years of age, I'm quite familiar with my weaknesses and strengths so I can quit tinkering with this or that melody and begin to play my own wonderful tune."

During our Men's Renewal weekend Jerry came to this powerful self-realization:

> *"I reject the hype in our culture which pressures us men to 'have it all.' There are lots of things I don't care about having or being. I now want to be discriminating in my life. I want to start pruning. I want to make choices about what's important to me, so I will grow as serenely and wisely as possible down the homestretch."*

I think about the poignant phrase in Langston Hughes' poem:

"When you turn the corner and you run into yourself, than you know that you have turned all the corners that are left."

We only live once, but if we live according to our own values and visions, once is enough.

XXVIII   *We want*
TO EMBRACE
AND BE EMBRACED

In a workshop on sexuality, men and women got to talking. Here is what we found out about one another.

Fundamentally, we hunger for the same qualities in sexual communion: detailed caring, spontaneity, openness to disparities in feeling, adventurousness, acceptance of yes's and no's, personal responsibility for making our sex interesting, emotional nourishment, and intellectual stimulation.

We also shared that we are more likely to turn ourselves off with fatigue, low self-esteem, and fears than be turned off by our partner.

None of us seemed to appreciate demeaning humor in our sex but did want plenty of genuinely lighthearted and fun-filled moments. Playfulness. Our sexual sharing is a serious matter, we agreed, but not a grim one.

We would all do well to touch one another with greater frequency, gentleness, and patience.

Second chances are essential.

Finally, what do you think constituted the height of sexual fulfillment for this group of males and females? Our almost unanimous response was: "An embrace...a warm, lingering embrace."

Some of the differences expressed that day were gender-based, but it was the sexual needs and hopes we shared in common that proved most heartening to the participants.

I followed up this workshop with male-only conversations about sexual desires. I invited men to elaborate on "the embrace" phenomenon. Here are some of their reflections.

One man said: "I hunger for an embrace from my sexual partner that surrounds me without engulfing me. The difference is subtle but real. I want to be caressed without being squeezed. I confess to being frightened by potential 'smothering' in my partnership."

Another man offered: "I want the embrace to precede sexual intercourse sometimes. Other times to follow it. Often the embrace can be the centerpiece of our closeness, neither leading to nor following after anything, just being the heart of our intimacy. It all depends."

Others talked about non-sexual touching. One man spoke of his exuberance upon feeling comfortable enough to hug other men without blushing or sweating. It was a healthy break-through in his maturing as a man.

A father coveted embraces with his children where he wasn't always the initiator. To be able to kiss them, gently and lovingly, now that they were teenagers was also something he treasured.

In an obscure biblical incident, King David, near death, was cold and frightened, even though he was fully clothed. The Old Testament reads: "He could not get warm." His servants found a woman to nurse him and lie on his bosom. There was no hint of overt sexuality in this gesture, only warmth and caring.

David died peacefully in the warmth of this tender touching.

This episode resembles what a chorus of men and women single out as crucial: embracing and being embraced.

New men are visualizing a world revolutionized by touch where women, men, and children engage, on a regular basis, in non-possessive, reassuring embraces.

XXIX *We want*
TO SHARE
OUR HOLY RELICS

    This may seem like an unusual passion, but I have heard it voiced by males in our new age. By holy relics I am not referring to artifacts purchased from a smiling concessioner in a European cathedral. Religious scholar Conrad Hyers recalls some relics that Martin Luther roundly rebuked:

> *"a tooth of John the Baptist, a piece of thread from Jesus' swaddling cloth, straw from the manger, a strand of Christ's beard, a crumb of bread from the Last Supper, slivers of wood from the cross, a twig from Moses' burning bush, a drop of milk from Mother Mary. The Archbishop*

of Mainz, not to be outdone,
claimed to have two feathers and an
egg from the Holy Ghost!"

From my perspective a relic is holy if
it serves as a source of creativity and
grounding in our lives. We cherish it; its
presence renews us.

In "Brother-Spirit" sessions we are
invited to place on the centering table
objects of meaning and sustenance.
Some of the presented tokens have been:

—a laughing Buddha which keeps
brother Alec awake and cheerful even
during difficult moments at work
—love-letters exchanged between
Mal and his father and brother sparking
deeper connections among the male
members of his family
—a candleholder made by a man
who had committed suicide...his artistry
and vision live on in his brother
—some desert artifacts brought
home by Lee following an excursion to
restore his spiritual equilibrium
—a precious children's picture book
that stirs pleasant family memories as
well as being a talisman of
encouragement in Phil's life

A professional friend of mine has
quotes stashed away in his wallet that he
pulls out and reads for spiritual snacks

during the day. He calls it "my wallet theology."

I remind men not to worship our relics but rather to respect and cherish them—then near the end of our lives, if at all possible, to pass them on to those we love.

Holy relics should never be sold or tossed.

XXX *We want* TO PUT A FACE ON OUR ENEMIES

"Don't introduce me to that person. I want to go on hating them, and I can't very well hate persons whom I have been introduced to and shared moments."

Charles Lamb

It may prove too much for some men to love, even accept or respect, their enemies, but to put faces on our foes is a bold, positive step toward greater understanding.

The art of putting a face on enemies is pertinent to interpersonal and interfamilial conflicts but especially challenging at the international level where most persons in seats of power are male.

American men have been conditioned to treat our enemies as

94

faceless, demonic creatures. Maintaining a hostile attitude toward our opposition has been our modus operandi. To make a peaceful move toward our enemies seems to throw our masculinity into question.

Let me remind you of what happened in President John F. Kennedy's regime. When Kennedy was poised to start thermonuclear war, his brother, the Attorney General, asked him to consider whether the American government or any government had the moral right to initiate nuclear war.

President Kennedy, I'm sorry to report, said he had no time to consider theories. He said that our country's "manhood," (yes, manhood was the word) demanded what he was about to do, though he must have known there would be little left of our land or its manhood or womanhood when he did. We were blessed to escape that close call back in 1962. Will there be a fire next time?

New men no longer believe in a world of absolute good (us) and absolute bad (them) which leads to the classic, deadly double standard where *our* missiles are justified but the missiles of our foes are evil.

Rod has come to this position:

"The Russians are not so much 'enemies' as 'strangers' we do not know. To put a face on our enemies, especially the Soviets, means to sit around the table and share what's on our hearts. That is the number one challenge on the human agenda. I am not a pacifist, but our very survival banks on a nuclear freeze of some sort."

Hans put it succinctly:

"Men have been leaders in fostering global hostilities; we now have to be moral leaders in bringing those hostilities to a halt. I feel a great responsibility to do my part in making that happen during my lifetime."

Paul challenged our Men's Fellowship to be more politically active in the peace movement when he said:

"Friends, fellow men, I hope you will join or support me at the Nevada test site protest next month. Combatting nuclear weapons will keep us morally sane."

An Israeli soldier in Lebanon said of

the people he was ordered to kill, "It's so hard when I'm up close. When I can see their faces, I can't bring myself to kill them. But when I'm farther away and am just shooting artillery shells, then I can do it."

A young American man in a missile silo, one of many with his finger on the nuclear button, said, "I don't know if I could kill anyone up close. This way I never have to see who my missile hits."

Daniel, a leader in our local Beyond War movement said:

"No one on earth is expendable, wherever they live, whatever system they espouse. We must teach our young children to tolerate, even appreciate, differences in other cultures. We must help our young children, especially boys, to outgrow war toys."

The momentum, the morale, the mission is present today for new men to be strong, vigorous peace-makers.

XXXI *We want*
TO LEARN THE ART
OF SURRENDER

"At some moment I did answer Yes to someone—or something—and from that hour I was certain that existence is meaningful and that, therefore, my life, in self-surrender, had a goal."

Dag Hammarskjöld

In men's growth and support experiences I have led over the past two decades, one of the universal deficiencies expressed was our dis-ease with surrendering: surrendering our money, our power, our time, our sexuality, our looks, our grudges, our dreams, you name it.

I'm no different than the majority of my brothers. I like to be in control of a situation, my destiny, others too.

98

We need patience on this matter. New men are bravely trying to relinquish things more easily—everything from our problems to our possibilities.

Some examples.

Mickey related: "I want to let my marriage be, to evolve more naturally than I tend to let it. I program our lives so tightly that I think I sometimes choke the juices out of my love for Vera."

Sam announced: "I don't want to career out of control, but I would gladly loosen some of the reins restricting my moves at work, at home, at play."

Harrison confessed: "I am struggling to learn the subtle, yet crucial, difference between surrender and capitulation, between letting go and giving up—a difference I feel will enhance my life markedly."

Surrender is a voluntary act; subjugation is coercive. As a marriage counselor I often invite couples to give themselves in love to one another without giving themselves away...neither to dominate nor be dominated by their partner but to live companionably alongside one another.

The art of surrendering means additional shifts for growing men.

First, with respect to children, it means that we fathers don't always have to be boss or be right. We can confess our ignorance and wrongs in front of our children without losing stature.

Second, with respect to other men, we can give up having to be better than "other guys." We can learn how to lose graciously as well as win gracefully.

Third, with respect to women, we can throw away the gender clubs we wield and participate in relationships of authentic give-and-take. We women and men hunger to abandon submitting and conquering strategies with one another and to engage in the lively art of mutual surrender.

Fourth, with respect to God, we men can pray in ways appropriate to our temperament and faith. We can stop using God to meet our ends. As Thomas Merton wrote:

> *"In place of manipulating, the man who prays stands receptive before the world. He no longer bites, but kisses; he no longer examines, but admires."*

New men foreswear patterns of

dominance, acknowledge that we don't always have to be top dogs or be in control of everything. If we can let go and let live, we end up being happier, healthier humans.

XXXII

We want TO BE RESPECTFUL ANIMALS

"First, be a good animal."

Ralph Waldo Emerson

Adam named the animals, but men have been slaying them ever since. We are the backbones of the National Rifle Association—hunters once by necessity, now by choice.

We have also perpetrated tragic experimentation with animals in fur ranches, factory farms, and laboratories.

There have been, to be sure, saints like St. Francis of Assisi who lived with wild animals and had the custom on Christmas eve of re-enacting the scene in an Italian barn. St. Francis believed in the

102

"peaceable kingdom" and practiced it among all living things.

The Jewish Midrash mentions how "both Moses and David were chosen to lead Israel because of their compassion toward animals."

And the Hindu holy man who refused heaven when he discovered that his faithful dog couldn't enter with him is another representative of respectfulness for animal kin.

But these men are the exceptions. Most of us have not treated animals as fellow creatures from whom we could learn much. It is not too late to change our ways. Earlier matriarchal societies treated humans, animals, and plants as equally sacred living realities.

Men will not become vegetarians overnight. Specieism will continue to rear its ugly head. But if we begin to practice basic respect toward our sister and brother animals, we will reclaim our own humanity as well. In brutalizing animals we are systematically de-humanized.

The highest ethic new males can pursue is full-fledged respect for all living things. We are co-inhabitants, not governors, of this wondrous planet. As the Russian novelist, Dostoevsky, wrote in *The Brothers Karamazov*:

> *"Love all God's creation, the whole universe, and each grain of sand. Love every leaflet, every ray of God's light; love the beasts, love the plants, love every creature. When you love every creature, you will understand the mystery of God in created things."*

After all, we humans *are* animals. Animal comes from "anima," meaning soul. Like all creatures we are alive, soul-filled, animated beings.

I encourage us men to be good, respectful animals ourselves by realizing our irrevocable kinship with all other animals who share the earth.

We bank on one another.

XXXIII *We want*
TO CONFRONT OUR FEARS

"Push fears out the front door, disown them or try to conquer them by will power and they will only return by the back door, like rejected children seeking love. I am the father of my fears; they will only depart when I have learned to accept them."

Sam Keen

As men we have been brought up to suppress and ignore rather than acknowledge and embrace our fears. We expend enormous energy projecting our anxieties onto external foes while we rarely deal with the demons inside our own souls, what Jesus called "the enemies within our own household."

Males are master projectionists—

pinning our hopes on outside governors, blaming our flaws on other individuals. We have played a major, sustaining role in the *isms* undermining our world today: racism, sexism, chauvinism. We have done this by an unwillingness to confront the tyrant, killer, oppressor that lurks in our dreams.

In men's groups one of the first challenges is for us to face our fears by confessing them. We say: "Okay, I'm scared. I admit it. Let me count the ways in which I'm frightened."

—"I'm scared of the deceit and mistrust circling in my mind."

—"I'm scared that I might be failing now with my children, my partnership, my friends or my work."

—"I'm scared that I might end up successful."

—"I'm scared of going too far, which keeps me from not going far enough in my commitments."

—"I'm scared because I seem to have lost my bearings."

—"I'm scared of dying."

I don't encourage men to erase our fears, even if we could. A living creature devoid of fear would be a psycho-spiritual freak. Fear is an essential piece of our innate survival equipment. Without fears we forfeit valuable life-experiences.

So we need to take care of our fears, be good to them; they can be our allies. As the Bible cautions: our purpose on earth is "to work out our salvation with fear and trembling."

Let me mention some good uses of healthy fear.

If we men were not anxious, we would not be yearning creatures. Anxiety is the discontent that moves us forward, keeps us adventurous. It is the goad that helps us to improve ourselves and make our world a lovelier place than it currently is. Fear, let's admit it, often motivates us into making necessary changes in our lives.

The same applies to love. The New Testament is wrong when it claims that "perfect love casts out fear." Love never rids us of our fears; it only enables us to live more effectively in the midst of them.

New males know that the greater the intimacy we risk with a companion, the scarier it can get. When we are honest, we both delight in and are terrified by the power we possess to harm one another.

Our hunger to be whole men means

recognizing, then befriending, scary characters in our emotional household. "Nice guys" who fail to deal with demons become shallow, even boring.

The words "sacred" and "scared" are almost identical, with two transposed letters. It's a fruitful twist because when we face what scares us, we are treading on sacred ground.

XXXIV *We want*
TO UNCLENCH OUR FISTS

*"All of my life I been like a doubled up fist...Poundin', smashin', drivin',—now I'm going to loosen these doubled up hands and touch things **easy** with them..."*

"Big Daddy" in Tennessee Williams' play "Cat On a Hot Tin Roof"

We all know that tension resides in our necks, backs, and stomachs, but I ask men to pay close attention to the posture and movement of their hands during the course of a grueling day. Numbers of men report that their hands roll into fists not only during stress-filled moments but even when they are home resting or watching TV. The tension is pervasive.

Clenched teeth, clenched fists— anything clenched— means that we men are leading angry, frustrated, tense lives and desperately hunger to vent, let go, unwind.

The rabbinical saying goes: "We come into this world with fists clenched, but when we die, our hands are open." The new male is not willing to wait until death before he unfolds his fists. He is beginning to open his heart and hands now in order to give and receive life's riches this side of the grave.

A daily exercise I encourage men to follow is called: "Palms Up/Palms Down."

It can be done upon rising, at midday or bedtime. You sit quietly, in a relaxed position, with your eyes closed.

Start by placing your palms up and saying: "I welcome into my life fresh, healing possibilities." Then, be calm for a few moments in a receiving mode.

Next put your palms down and utter: "I empty my life of the vengeful, bitter, nagging feelings which hold me in their grasp. Palms down to them. I let them go."

Continue this process, alternating

between palms up and palms down until your heart is invigorated and mind stilled.

It works, brothers, and takes only minutes.

XXXV *We want*
TO SHARE
COM-PANIONSHIP

"When I hear bread breaking I see something else; it seems almost as though God never meant us to do anything else. So beautiful a sound, the crust breaks up like manna and falls all over everything, and then we eat. Bread gets inside humans!"

Daniel Berrigan

A com-panion literally means "one who eats bread with another."

For centuries men focused on *earning* bread in competition rather than *breaking* bread in fellowship. There is something primal and precious about the gatherings new men share in wilderness cabins or tents where we cook meals communally, then with laughter interspersed amid the crunching of food .

112

and silence...we enjoy profound companionship.

Eating is near the heart of religion. In the Old Testament, wherever you turn, God is either sitting down to table or setting one up for others. The Last Supper is a celebration full of affection, food, betrayal, remembrance, hope, and anxiety. The kingdom of God is described as a huge banquet hall. People arrive from the North, South, East, and West, sit down, bridge their foreignness, and feast together.

Breaking bread together is an utterly natural gesture like a smile, an embrace, a wave of the hand. To eat at a common table means recognition of relationship, of ties that bind us in a mysterious unity, of mutual care and shared responsibility.

The Gaelic word for family means "those who eat together." When we cut ourselves off from shared, sacred meals, we cut ourselves off from kin.

Whenever new men sit down to eat together, we remember the past, reflect upon our future, and revel in our present. When we break open a loaf of bread, we are breaking open our lives in trust. When we pour from a bottle of refreshment, we are pouring ourselves forth in affection.

113

XXXVI *We want*
TO PRACTICE FORGIVENESS

"Forgiveness is not an impulse that is in much favor. The prevalent style in the world runs more to the high-plains drifter, to the hard, cold eye of the avenger, to a numb remorselessness. Forgiveness does not look much like a tool for survival in a bad world. But that is what it is."

Lance Morrow

New males hunger for forgiveness.

Frank confided in me:

"I have enough money, power, and sex to make me feel settled and secure, but I don't. I'm restless. What I really want is the farthest thing from my grasp. I hunger for some peace: peace with my loved ones, peace with my place in the universe, mainly peace with myself.

114

*To accomplish this I am going to
have to begin forgiving and being
forgiven.*"

Frank made the necessary amends
to produce greater serenity. He had
spent most of his life acquiring,
producing, climbing like most men. His
talents were many, but his spirit was
malnourished. Frank came to realize that
spiritual fulfillment was his true goal and
that "forgiveness was his deepest need
and highest achievement."

We have been programmed since
boyhood to pretend that we are
unaffected by other people's cruelty—
deliberate or accidental—in short, we are
programmed to bypass forgiveness.

But the times are changing. So are
men. Although we have paid an
exorbitant price for failing to forgive and
be forgiven, there is news of encouraging
breakthroughs in the male world.

Peter, depressed by feelings of
inadequacy, finally forgave his father's
relentless pressure and is now able not
only to lead a freer life but to relate to his
father with more affection.

Olaf told me that his life had been
essentially contaminated, if not
dominated, by unexpressed resentments

115

toward his older sister. At the age of sixty-seven he was ready to forfeit pride and surrender resentment in order to achieve reconciliation with her. He said: "Forgiveness costs a lot, but refusing to forgive extracts an even higher payment."

William wrote two letters, one to his former wife and another to her parents both asking for forgiveness and sharing forgiveness for the unresolved hurts surrounding his painful divorce.

He asked for no reply; he didn't receive any, but he now lives a freer life because of *his* willingness to risk those cleansing messages.

Dennis learned that forgiveness is just as hard to receive as to give. He realized this when he repeatedly rejected his son's offer of forgiveness. He had been getting emotional mileage out of harboring a grudge against his offspring. He finally opened up his heart to his son's gift.

The truth is that bitterness never puts us in control; instead it places us in bondage to our resentment. As the Chinese proverb notes: "The one who pursues revenge should dig two graves."

Abe learned the toughest lesson of all: self-forgiveness. Sometimes we treat

116

others more compassionately than we do ourselves. We wind up holding ourselves hostage by failing to forgive ourselves. He said: "I now can acknowledge that I am more than any of my mistakes, however grievous they may have been. I am learning to accept myself and begin again."

Men, we have three choices: avoidance, resentment, or forgiveness. Given those options, only the latter one can bring our lives release and refreshment over the long haul and move us nearer a holy and loving life.

XXXVII *We want* **TO CREATE BROTHER-SPIRIT**

Women tend to be more evolved than men in matters of the spirit. The field of feminist theology is flourishing.

Men remain in a quandary. We can't accept the stifling, demeaning, sexist imagery and substance of patriarchal religion that has been both oppressive to women and undermining of authentic maleness. The new male is interested neither in subjugating himself to a supernatural being nor in dominating women on earth.

However, new men can't merely react to or build upon feminist thought. It doesn't speak directly to our experience.

118

Our male identity will be uncertain until we establish a version of spirituality that grows out of the soil of male pride, pain, and possibility. Courses I have led in Brother-Spirit are one such attempt. In the course we focus on intimacy *and* ultimacy. Through personal sharing we move toward making peace—deep, enduring peace—in four primary areas: with ourselves, our neighbors, the natural world, and divine reality.

We clarify the meanings in our lives of sacred time and space, of ritual, symbol, and silence, of death and immortality.

In our ongoing Brother-Spirit odyssey we take serious spiritual stock of our lives by asking tough, stretching questions like: Whose am I? *or* To whom do I belong? What is my special task or calling while on this earth? Who will be my spiritual fellow-travelers for the journey?

These, along with others, are unanswerable questions. We know that. We can only dance with them, but in so dancing, our hearts are stirred, our minds pushed, our spirits fed.

XXXVIII *We want* **TO FIND, THEN FOLLOW, OUR GOD**

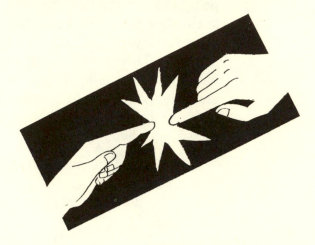

"Hear, O Israel: the Lord our God is one Lord; and you shall love the Lord your God with all your heart, and with all your soul, and with all your might."

Deuteronomy 6:4

My interpretation of the Old Testament passage is that we humans must make a personal decision about the nature of the god/God we will serve. We are to love *our* God not someone else's. This is challenging news to so many men who have grown up living in allegiance to an inherited deity.

Instead, once we have made our

own choices, we are charged to give our total selves in devotion to a higher reality—using heart, soul, and might in loyalty to this power.

As my colleague, Scotty, noted: "The key question is not whether God exists, but who or what is *my* God?" What is my ultimate concern in life? Who/what force or presence holds my life together during the dark nights, happy days, and in-between blahs?

Martin Luther put the issue clearly centuries ago: "Whatever thy heart clings to and relies upon, that is properly *thy* God."

In this process I encourage men to worry about deeds of goodness and less about creeds concerning God. God wants us to be focused on human not godly things, on economic justice more than metaphysics. Elie Wiesel says: "God is telling us—'I can take care of my own ideas, images, theories—you take care of my creation.'"

Confucius doesn't chatter about God, Buddha says that theological raps about the "unknown" don't edify the spirit, and Zen Buddhists remain silent. New men who are inclined to be quiet about God or love in response to the Creator rather than discourse upon or debate about deity move in fine, religious company.

Since our family trip to the Sistine
Chapel in Rome two years ago, I can't
get out of my mind the powerful panel in
Michelangelo's creation depicting God
and Adam.

Adam raises an arm toward God,
whose arm, in turn, extends toward the
new human. Index fingers on both hands
move toward each other, but they do not
quite touch.

Humanity *and* divinity are stretching
to make connection. The religious life is
lived in that gap where we reach but do
not ultimately grasp one another...in the
almost, the between.

Shortly before his death, a great
Indian chief was asked the secret of his
tribe's success. He answered, "We were
a disorganized tribe, as you know, but we
were on pretty good terms with the
Great Spirit."

New men are beginning to accept
the challenge to stay on pretty good
terms with the highest and best we know.
We want our behavior to match our
beliefs. We want to align our ways with
whatever god we choose to honor. We
never want to hurt anyone, including
ourselves, fighting over versions of an
elusive, mysterious presence we dare to
call divine.

122

XXXIX *We want*
TO CONSENT TO DIE

"Life is the destiny we are bound to refuse until we have consented to die."

W. H. Auden

My father wasn't around the house much as his children were growing up. He worked long and hard, too long and hard. But when he was home, he was present. He was tangible, touching. He affirmed us boys with his hugging, the feel of his grizzly beard, and his warm, sturdy hand.

I will never forget my father's indistinguishable odor. Mothers and babies sense it; same with lovers. I had it with my Dad whenever we kissed.

All this was enough to grow on.

Although Dad took good care of our

family, upon his death, I irrationally blurted out: "Who will take care of my brother, Phil, and me now? Who will bring home the food? Who will handle my insurance policies? Who will allow me to be a boy? How can I remain a son without a father?"

My father's death was no less anguishing because he was eighty-one. It was the only death he will ever have. He was the only father I ever had.

I won't forget Harold Alexander Towle. He's dead, but I won't lose him. In the play entitled "I Never Sang for My Father" there is an unforgettable line: "Death ends a life but not a relationship, which struggles on in the mind of the survivor toward some resolution."

There is a piercing Navaho phrase which resounds in my heart: "My father died; he left me the earth." That's how I feel now that my father is gone. I have to contend with the entire earth. I am now one of those in charge. I am next in line to die.

I will do fine, but the child in me never wanted it to happen this way. My father was invincible, wasn't he? My primitive longing was to have one or both of my parents present when I took my final breath just as they were there for my first one.

124

We all are vulnerable before the mysteries of death and dying. There is no man who does not stand naked, ignorant, virginal, and somewhat squeamish before his final disappearance into darkness.

We men resist the possibility of our own death so fiercely that we are often unable to live. We spend the bulk of our time avoiding our demise so we have little energy and focus left over for embracing existence.

Only when we consent to die—that is, admit our own cessation, make peace with our own death—are we able to soar while on this earth.

Henry David Thoreau wrote: "I wish to learn what life has to teach, and not, when I come to die, discover that I have not lived." Some men, due to fear and bitterness, live dying. Others, due to joy and thankfulness, die living.

My father died living. That's the challenge of my second half of existence.

XL *We want*
TO LEAVE
A LASTING LEGACY

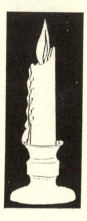

*"I want to be thoroughly used up when I
die, for the harder I work, the more I live.
Life is no brief candle for me. It is a sort of
splendid torch which I have got hold of for
the moment, and I want to make it burn as
brightly as possible before handing it on to
future generations."*

—George Bernard Shaw

When men explore beneath their
ostensible desires to be wealthy,
Casanovas, and top dogs, we find our
pivotal, secret aspiration: to spend our
lives for something which will outlast us!

I have led numerous discussions
where I ask men, point blank: "When the
dust settles, when you are gone, how do

126

you wish to be remembered?"

Here is a sampling of their responses.

Dale said:

"I want to be known as a good son to my parents, a faithful father to my children, and a loving mate. That's it. There's nothing fancy or startling about my deepest desires."

Max spoke to our group as follows:

"Writing may be my best way to pass something on. The poems I've composed during my lifetime will never be published for the outside world. I don't really care. But my children have promised to keep them in the family as heirlooms for my children's children's children. I don't think they will be taken to the dump for a few generations anyway."

George phrases his final wishes this way:

"I want my remains scattered on this property because I built this house with my own two hands, and even if it burns down, I will still be

*here in spirit. That's all I want you
to remember about me: a loving
builder."*

Grant reflected:

*"I remember my father always giving
time, energy, and affection to
others—running errands of
kindness. My goal for the remainder
of my life is to be like him. At his
memorial service one friend stood
up and said something I have never
forgotten: 'Jack was the kind of
person whom you could not see on
the street without wondering on
what loving errand he was going.'
Well, it will be more than enough if
someone stands up at my memorial
service and says something like that
about good old Grant."*

My friend Merv is a sculptor who
has never married. He is about as
creative a person as I know, yet he never
sired children. His sculptures are his
offspring. He quoted Rilke when I asked
him about his immortality and legacy:

*"Perhaps overall there is a great
motherhood as a common
longing. . .and even in the man there
is motherhood, it seems to me,*

*physical and spiritual; his
procreating is also a kind of giving
birth and giving birth it is when he
creates out of inmost fulness."*

Merv went on to say: "I try to create
my sculpture out of my inmost fulness."

There is no man I have met,
interviewed, or counseled who does not
want to pass on some legacy to future
generations. The gifts may vary, but the
desire to achieve personal immortality
seems to be fundamental. As Daniel
Levinson writes:

*"The wish for immortality is one of
the strongest and least malleable of
human motives. Although the real
value of a man's legacy is impossible
to measure, in his mind it defines to
a large degree the ultimate value of
his life—and his claim on
immortality."*

Our task as new males, then, is to
pinpoint those attributes and creations
which we wish to pass on. This stock-
taking process will help us be more self-
governing and accountable for our
legacies—prioritizing our time and
efforts.

Clare Booth Luce wrote: "A great

129

person is one sentence. History has no time for more than one sentence, and it is always a sentence that has an active verb."

It is crucial for new men to become aware of our own mortality, to begin to shape our primary sentence, to find our verb, and then to keep the sentence in front of our mind's eye.

We become who we are now becoming.

A MAN-IFESTO

Dear Men,

I invite you to post this manifesto at your work station, on your bathroom mirror, in your wallet, or carve it in your heart's memory.

"I AM A MAN—ALWAYS WAS AND ALWAYS WILL BE.

I WON'T FIGHT MY NATURE. I WON'T FORFEIT MY DESTINY. I WON'T SHY AWAY FROM MAKING MANIFEST THE SPECIAL MALE PERSON I WAS CREATED TO BE AND BECOME.

I AM HERE ON EARTH FOR A SHORT WHILE TO LIVE A HOLY, CARING, ACTUALIZED EXISTENCE.

I WILL BE THE FREEST AND FULLEST SELF POSSIBLE DURING MY STAY.

I WILL LIVE PROUDLY, BRAVELY, AND LOVINGLY AS A NEW MAN.

Your buddy,
Tom

Mail Order Information:

For additional copies of *New Men—Deeper Hungers* send $7.95 per book plus $1.50 for shipping and handling (ADD 6% Sales Tax-CA Res.). Make checks payable to Tom-Owen-Towle, 3303 Second Avenue, San Diego, California 92103. Telephone (619) 295-7067.

☐ NEW MEN—DEEPER HUNGERS, $7.95
☐ GENERATION TO GENERATION, $7.95
☐ STAYING TOGETHER, $7.95

Also available through local bookstores that use R.R. Bowker Company BOOKS IN PRINT catalogue system. Order through publisher SUNFLOWER INK for bookstore discount.